heritage from the kitchen: a doucet hennessy house recipe book

Edited by **patsy hennessy**

Edited by **rolande doucet-o'connell**

Edited by **rod o'oconnell**

Edited by **melynda jarratt**

Edited by **lucy jarratt**

Heritage From The Kitchen: A Doucet Hennessy House Recipe Book / by AMDHHA Inc.

ISBN 978-1-989621-08-0 (Print)

ISBN 978-1-989621-09-7 (E-book)

1. COOKING / History. 2. HISTORY / Canada / Provincial, Territorial & Local / Atlantic Provinces (NB, NL, NS, PE). 3. COOKING / Courses & Dishes / Desserts. 4. COOKING / Courses & Dishes / Soups & Stews. I. AMDHHA Inc., author.

Published by The Hennessy Entertainment Company | HennessyEnt.com

contents

about this recipe book

Every family has its favourite recipes that are passed down from one generation to another. And so it is with the Doucets and Hennessys. The Association Maison Doucet Hennessy Association Inc., has compiled this recipe book as a fundraising project for 2012. Throughout the summer of 2011 we asked for submissions from everyone with connections to the house in order to get as many recipes as possible. In this book you will find tried and true recipes for sweets, breads and main dishes that have passed the test of time. Bon appétit and thank you for supporting our plans to restore this historic house at 375 St Peter Avenue, Bathurst, New Brunswick.

Chaque famille possède ses recettes préférées qui ont été transmises d'une génération à l'autre. Il en est ainsi avec les familles Doucet et Hennessy. L'Association Doucet Hennessy Association Inc. a compilé ce livre de recettes comme un des projets de levée de fonds pour l'année 2012. Au courant de l'été 2011, nous avons demandé à tous et chacun qui avaient des liens avec la maison ou avec les familles Doucet et Hennessy de nous soumettre des recettes afin d'en recueillir autant que possible. Dans ce livre vous trouverez des recettes testées et approuvées pour des pâtisseries, des pains, et des plats principaux. Bon appétit et merci de nous appuyer dans nos plans pour restaurer cette maison historique au 375 avenue St-Pierre, Bathurst, Nouveau-Brunswick.

AMDHHA Inc.
375 St. Peter Ave.
Bathurst, NB • E2A 2Y4
Email: info@DoucetHennessy.com
Web: www.DoucetHennessy.com
Charitable Reg.#: 817923261RR0001

sweets, muffins, pastries & breads

. . .

Petites douceurs, muffins, pâtisseries et pains

Recipes appear in the language they were submitted.
Les recettes paraissent dans la langue dans laquelle elles ont été soumises.

biscuits chauds à priscille

Soumis par Rolande Doucet O'Connell.

Ingredients

- A peu près 2 tasses de farine
- 1/4 tasse de sucre
- 2 cuillerées à thé de poudre à pâte
- 3/4 cuillerée à thé de sel
- 1/2 tasse saindoux ou margarine
- 1 tasse de lait

Directions

Priscille (Frenette) Doucet a écrit son autobiographie qui a été publiée sous le titre: Enracinée comme l'Arbre, 2003.

1. Mettre le farine, sucre, poudre à pâte, et sel dans tamis. Tamiser le tout dans un bol.
2. Ajouter 1/2 tasse saindoux ou margarine. Défaire le gras dans la farine avec les mains.
3. Ajouter une tasse de lait.
4. Mélanger les ingrédients secs avec le lait jusqu'à l'obtention d'une pâte molle (ne pas trop travailler la pâte).
5. Abaisser la pâte avec un rouleau à pâte à 3/4 de pouce d'épaisseur.
6. Découper la pâte à l'aide d'un petit verre (2" de diamètre).
7. Cuire sur une plaque à biscuits de 12 à 15 minutes dans un four préchauffé à 350°F.

"Le 27 mai 1936, lendemain de notre mariage qui a eu lieu à l'église Sainte-Thérèse de Robertville, Gilbert se lève à 7 heures, charge le ménage à bord du truck à cheval et sîen va le livrer à Sormany, une distance dí à peine 5 milles. Il ne revient qu'à 7 heures du soir. Le 28 au matin, il fallait encore faire le même trajet avec le truck, charger les boîtes ainsi que ma grosse valise. Aller jusqu'à Val Michaud, le chemin était bon. A partir de là, il y avait seulement quelques années que le chemin était ouvert. C'avait été fait à la pioche et la pelle depuis 1934. Plusieurs colons vivaient là dans des camps comme le nôtre. Le chemin était bon pour marcher ou à cheval et truck, mais pas pour une jeune mariée. On s'est bien rendus jusqu'à chez Edmond L. Boudreau. Moi j'étais assise sur ma grosse valise quand la roue du truck a tombé dans un trou de vase. J'ai tombé enbas. J'étais en *petits souliers. Je pensais que j'arrivais à New York! J'ai été à la maison et Mme Boudreau m'a passé une paire de bottes pour me rendre à mon camp. Je me suis bien rendue et je n'ai pas sorti pour un mois. J'étais bien arrivée au camp. Il fallait dîner. J'ai fait ma recette de biscuits chauds qui était ma spécialité (et qui l'est encore jusqu'à ce jour, (2003) selon mes enfants)."*

Extrait du livre: Enracinée comme l'Arbre (2003), p. 39, Priscille Frenette Doucet (1915-2007)

Augustin Frenette et son épouse (Doucet) Philomène dans une photo prise en 1902. Philomène était la fille d'Aimé et Marie (Roy) Doucet. Aimé était le fils de Charles (Charlo) Doucet et Marie (Pélagie) Lejeune de Petit-Rocher. "Charlo" était le fils de Michel et Anne (Boudreau) Doucet de Bathurst-Ouest et un pionnier de Petit-Rocher. Michel était le fils de Charles (Charlitte) et Anne (Arseneault) Doucet de Beaubassin, Nouvelle-Écosse. "Charlitte" est décédé en 1798 dans l'ouest de Bathurst, huit ans après que lui et son fils Charles Jr. aient pétitionné le roi d'Angleterre, George III, pour une concession de terre de ce qui était alors Nepisiquit. Il se passera encore onze années avant que le rêve de cette famille acadienne de posséder des terres dans Nepisiquit, se réalise. Ils reçurent le Titre de propriété #12 en 1807. L'année suivante, ils construisirent une maison au même endroit où est située la Maison Doucet Hennessy aujourd'hui. Photo gracieuseté de Clare O'Connell Noon.

butterscotch squares

Submitted by Lucy (Hennessy) Jarratt

Square Ingredients

- 1 cup brown sugar
- 1/2 cup butter or margarine
- 1 egg, well beaten
- 1 tsp vanilla
- 1 cup flour
- 1 tsp baking powder
- 1/2 tsp salt
- 1/2 cup walnuts chopped

Patrick and Beatrice (Moran) Hennessy pose for a photo with their four children and Moran relatives outside the Doucet Hennessy House, circa 1919. Two year old Lucy is at bottom, in her mother's lap.

Fudge Icing Ingredients

- 1 cup brown sugar
- 1/2 cup white sugar
- A few grains of salt
- 1/3 cup milk or cream
- 2 tbsp corn syrup
- 1 tsp vanilla

Square Directions

1. Melt sugar and butter. Let cool.
2. Add vanilla, well beaten egg and sifted dry ingredients mixed with walnuts. Beat well.
3. Spread in a buttered pan (8x8 inches). Bake 350°F for 20 min.
4. When cool spread with Fudge Icing. Cut in squares.

Icing Directions

1. Mix all and bring slowly to boiling point.
2. Cook 5 - 10 minutes.
3. Add vanilla.
4. Let stand for a few minutes, then beat until creamy and ready to spread on squares.

Lucy (Hennessy) Jarratt was born in the Doucet Hennessy House on June 29, 1917. Except for a short period when she lived on Murray Avenue with her husband and ailing mother- in-law, Alice Jarratt, Lucy has lived in or near the family homestead her entire life. In the early 1960s, she and her husband Sidney built a house at the top of what is now Hennessy Street, in Hennessy Subdivision. Lucy and Sidney had nine children; Billy, Sally, Anne, Snooker, Peter, Johnny, Theresa, David and Melynda.

Manus R. Kane and Lucy (Hennessy) Jarratt in a photo taken outside the Doucet Hennessy House circa 1919. Manus Kane was Beatrice (Moran) Hennessy's uncle and he bought the Doucet House from Father William Varrily, the priest at Holy Family Church. Father Varrily came into possession of the Doucet house through Marie (Hachey) McManus, the granddaughter of Charles Doucet, after her husband, Hon. Francis McManus, a former Member of the Legislature for Gloucester, passed away in 1897. Varrily Street in Hennessy Subdivision is named after Father Varrily. Beatrice and Patrick Hennessy named one of their children Varrily, in honour of the priest. Photo from the Hennessy Fonds, Provincial Archives of New Brunswick.

carrés au chocolat et guimauve

Soumis par Clara (Morrison) Doucet.

Ingredients

- 1/2 tasse beurre
- 2 carrés chocolat
- 1 tasse sucre blanc
- 2 œufs
- 1/2 cuillerée à thé vanille
- 3/4 tasse farine
- 1/2 cuillerée à thé poudre à pâte
- 1/4 cuillerée à thé sel
- 3/4 1 noix hachées
- 20 guimauves

Clara Doucet et son mari Jean Guy dans une photo récente.

Ingrédients glaçage

- 3 cuillerées à table beurre
- 2 tasses sucre à glaçage
- 2 carrés chocolat
- 1/4 tasse de lait
- 1/2 cuillerée à thé vanille
- 1 pincée sel

Directions carrés

1. Faire fondre le beurre et le chocolat. Ajouter le sucre, ensuite les œufs et bien mélanger ensemble.
2. Ajouter les ingrédients secs ensemble. Mélanger avec la vanille et les noix.
3. Cuire dans un plat 9 x 12 à 350°F pour 18 à 20 minutes.
4. Couper les guimauves en trois parties chacune.
5. Enlever les carrés du four lorsqu'ils sont cuits et les couvrir de guimauves. Retournez-les au four pour 5 minutes. Laisser refroidir.
6. Ensuite, couvrir de glaçage.

Directions glaçage

1. Faire fondre le chocolat et le beurre ensemble. Ajouter le lait, la vanille et le sel.
2. Mélanger avec le sucre à glaçage et bien le brasser.

Recette de Berthilde Arseneau Doucet, Èpouse de Norman L. Doucet. Ils étaient tous deux de très bons cuisiniers.

La famille ne pourra jamais oublier tous ces bons repas dégustés ensemble autour de la table. Parents de dix enfants, cinq garçons et cinq filles.

carrés aux dates

Soumis par Clara (Morrison) Doucet

Ingrédients

- 1 lb de dattes hachées
- 1 tasse de cassonade
- 1 tasse d'eau ou plus
- 1 cuillerée à thé de vanille
- 1 cuillerée à table de beurre

Pâte Ingrédients

- 1 3/4 tasse de farine d'avoine
- 1 tasse de cassonade
- 3/4 tasse de margarine ou beurre
- 3/4 cuillerée à thé de soda
- 1 3/4 tasses de farine
- 1 pincée de sel

Directions

1. Cuire à feu doux les ingrédients pour la garniture ensuite ajouter 1 cuillerée à thé de vanille et 1 cuillerée à table de beurre. Laisser refroidir.
2. Mélanger le beurre, le sucre et la farine d'avoine ensemble. Ajouter la farine et le soda. Bien mélanger le tout du bout des doigts.
3. Diviser la pâte en deux parties et en placer une au fond d'un plat graissé. Ensuite placer la garniture au dessus et placer l'autre partie de la pâte au dessus de la garniture.
4. Cuire 15 minutes à 375°F et 10 à 15 minutes à 325°F.

Recette de Clara Morrison Doucet, épouse de Jean-Gu y Doucet, fils de Norman et Berthilde Doucet. Moi, Clara, je suis la fille de James Morrison d'une descendance Ecossaise Èpoux de Vélina Roy d'une descendance Acadienne. Je suis la neuvième d'une famille de 20 enfants dont 15 filles et cinq garçons de Beresford au Nouveau-Brunswick. Faisant suite à ma recette, y parait que je suis la meilleure faiseuse de carrés aux dattes de toute ma famille. Je trouve cela spécial car cette recette je l'ai créé en suivant des conseils de ma mère, ma belle mère et en employant mes propres idées. Tout pour vous rassurer que toute personne qui veut, peut créer ses propres recettes, il faut d'abord être à l'Ècoute, prendre des conseils et foncer, bonne chance!!!

Milieu à gauche: La famille de l'Hon. Francis McManus et son épouse Marie (Hachey). Marie était la fille de Hilarion Hachey et Marie (Doucet). Le grand-père maternel de Marie McManus, Charles Doucet, est celui qui a construit la maison originale vers 1808. Suite au décès de Francis McManus en 1897, la Maison Doucet Hennessy est entrée en possession du révérend William Varrily, le curé de l'église Sainte-Famille. Photo gracieuseté de Mme Florence Roussy.

delphine's coconut bread

Submitted by Bev (Doucet) Jarratt

Ingredients

- Butter - size of an egg
- 1 cup white sugar
- 1 egg
- 2 cups flour
- 2 tsp baking powder
- 1/2 tsp salt
- 1 cup milk
- 1 cup shredded coconut, or substitute orange peeling

Melynda Jarratt and Beverly (Doucet) Jarratt in a photo taken in July, 2010.

Directions

1. Let stand for 20 minutes before baking.
2. Bake for 1 hour at 375°F.

Beverly (Doucet) Jarratt is the daughter of Ralph and Lorraine (Christie) Doucet. She married Albert Charles "Peter" Jarratt in 1984 and they lived in the Doucet Hennessy House for two years after they were married. Bev has a step-daughter, Alisson Grenon-Bent, and a son, Peter M. Jr. Bev is the proud grandmother of Lilyan, Reese, Payton and Kersten. This recipe was a favourite of Bev's aunt, Delphine Doucet.

elsie's date squares

Submitted by Lucy (Hennessy) Jarratt

Filling Ingredients

- 1 1/3 cups dates
- 3 tbsp white sugar
- 1 tsp lemon juice

Base Ingredients

- 2 cups oatmeal
- 1 cup brown sugar
- 2 cups flour
- 1 tsp soda
- 1 tsp salt
- 1 cup shortening or butter or margarine

Leah Blackmore, Lucy Jarratt, Maggie Watson and Elsie Bald win at a CWL event in 1985.

Filling Directions

1. Cover dates with water and bring to a boil, then simmer until liquid is absorbed, stirring constantly.
2. Take off stove.
3. Add the white sugar and lemon juice. Mix well and let cool.

Base Directions

1. Mix well. Put half in an 8 x 13 pan. Cover with date filling and then rest of base.
2. Cook at 350 degrees Fahrenheit for 20 minutes or 400 for 10 minutes.
3. Let cool and cut in squares.

This was Elsie (Doucet) Baldwin's favourite recipe but knowledge of how to make her famous date squares was strictly on a need-to-know basis. Only a few of her very closest friends ever managed to get the recipe in writing before she passed away: so when you make these date squares keep in mind that this recipe used to be considered top secret!

papa's doughnuts

Submitted by Michael Hennessy

Ingredients

- 1/4 cup shortening
- 1 cup milk
- 2 eggs
- 1 cup sugar
- 1 1/2 tsp soda
- 3 tsp cream of tartar
- 3/4 tsp ginger
- Flour - add enough so dough is soft (3+ cups).

Patrick Hennessy, his youngest child Robert "Bobby" and eldest daughter Lucy on December 9, 1940. This photo was taken in the front yard of the Doucet Hennessy House.

Directions

1. Chill dough.
2. Cook in deep fryer at 400°F
3. You can also use Mazola oil in a frying pan as well.
4. It takes 1-2 minutes on each side.

Patrick Hennessy was born in Blackville in 1884, the son of William and Mary Anne (Vickers) Hennessy. He married Beatrice Moran in 1911 and they had nine children; Manus, Roger, Lucy, Anna, James, Dorothy, Varrily, Bruno and Robert. A logging cook by trade, he served overseas during the Second World War with the Canadian Forestry Corps. Young "Bobby" in the photo above grew up to be Dr. Robert Hennessy and Robert's youngest son Michael, submitted t his recipe in memory of Patrick. Michael is a founding Board Member of the AMDHHA Inc.

hot water pastry

Submitted by Ruth Comeau

Ingredients

- 1 lb Tenderflake lard - room temperature
- 1 cup boiling water - or meat broth if making meat pies
- 1 tbsp caraway seeds (optional)
- 6 cups flour (keep 1 for rolling)
- 3 tsp baking powder
- 2 tsp salt

Directions

Ruth Comeau with her trusty rolling pin, August 2011.

1. In a large bowl, chunk up lard and pour in boiling liquid. Blend completely - a potato masher works.
2. Cool to room temperature, stirring frequently to prevent fat from separating.
3. Mix 5 cups flour with baking powder and salt.
4. Dump 1/2 into liquid - stir well.
5. Dump in other 1/2 - stir well.
6. Cover with damp towel and refrigerate 1-2 hours, or overnight.
7. To use - break off a piece (1/6), work it in your hands to soften enough to roll.
8. Flour work surface and roll to desired thickness. Makes 3 double crusts.

Ruth Comeau is a family friend of the Jarratts and she makes a mean pastry!

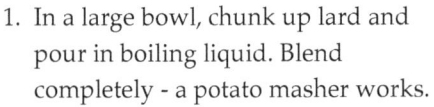

jello cake

Submitted by Corinne (Comeau) Hebert

Ingredients

- 2 packages of Strawberry Jello (Light)
- 1 angel food cake

Directions

Left to right: Régis Comeau, Edgar Comeau, Corinne Hebert, Thérèse Hennessy, Hélène Williams. February, 1995.

1. Mix jello as directed and cut up the cake, mix in with jello.
2. Put in fridge. Keeps well for a while, very good.
3. Add Dream Whip or ice cream when serving.

Corrine (Comeau) Hebert is the sister of Thérèse (Comeau) Hennessy.

nanny's johnny cake

Submitted by Patricia Hennessy

Ingredients

- 1 1/2 cup flour
- 2 tsp baking powder
- 3/4 tsp baking soda
- 1 tsp salt
- 2 tbsp sugar
- 1 cup corn meal
- 2 eggs
- 1 1/4 cup sour milk
- 3 tbsp melted butter

Beatrice and Patrick Hennessy on their 50th wedding anniversary in 1961. This photo was taken on the lawn of the Doucet Hennessy House.

Directions

1. Mix together: flour, baking powder, baking soda, salt.
2. Add sugar, corn meal. Mix thoroughly.
3. Beat eggs and sour milk together until light. Use to moisten dry ingredients.
4. Stir in melted butter.
5. Pour into greased pan 8 x 8 x 2.
6. Bake in hot oven at 425°F for 40 minutes.

Patsy is the oldest of the Hennessy grandchildren and spent most of her working career in the Royal Canadian Navy, retiring in 1989 after 21 years of service. Since that time she has occupied her time with genealogy research which she finds fascinating and rewarding. She is the founding co-President of the AMDHHA Inc.

lemon squares

Submitted by Anne Marie Doucet

Bottom Ingredients

- 1 cup flour
- 2 tbsp brown sugar
- 1/2 cup Butter
- 2 tsp salt

Top Ingredients

- 1 1/2 cups coconut
- 1 cup white sugar
- 2 tbsp flour
- Pinch of salt
- Rind and juice of 1 lemon
- 2 Eggs

Anne Marie Doucet, volunteer extraordinaire, helps stuff envelopes for the Association Maison Doucet Hennessy House Association.

Bottom Directions

1. Mix together, spread in 9x9 inch pan, cook for 10 minutes at 350°F.

Top Directions

1. Mix together, pour over bottom, cook for 10-15 minutes at 350°F.
2. Top with icing sugar.

Anne Marie Doucet was born in Bathurst in 1959, the eldest child of Lorraine (Christie) and Ralph Doucet. She has three siblings, Robert, Bev and Sandra. Anne Marie is a valued member of the Holy Family Church Catholic Womens League and the Church Choir.

mom's molasses ginger cookies

Submitted by Clare (O'Connell) Noon

Ingredients

- 1 cup (250mL) shortening
- 1 cup (250mL) sugar
- 1 cup (250mL) molasses
- 5 cups (5x250mL) flour
- 2 tsp (10mL) ground ginger
- 1 tsp (5mL) ground cinnamon
- 1/2 tsp (2mL) ground cloves
- 1 tsp (5mL) salt
- 2 tsp (10mL) baking soda dissolved in 1/2 cup of boiling water then fill cup with cold water

Ezella (Frenette) and Gerald O'Connell on their wedding day, August 1, 1939, LaTuque, Québec.

Directions

1. Mix all ingredients well and then chill.
2. Preheat oven to 375°F (190°C).
3. Roll out dough and cut with cookie cutter.
4. Bake for about 8 minutes.

Ezella (Frenette) O'Connell (1913-2000) was born in Robertville, NB. She married Gerald O'Connell (1909-2000) and together they raised four children; Clare, Rod, Paul and Kevin. They resided on St. Anne St. in West Bathurst on a lot purchased from Beatrice Hennessy. Her paternal grandmother was Philomène Doucet wife of Augustin Frenette. This recipe was submitted by Clare (O'Connell) Noon in her mother's memory.

muffins aux bananes et à l'ananas

Soumis par Diane David

Ingrédients

Diane David, COSL 1987-89.

- 3 tasses farine tout usage 750 ml
- 2 tasses sucre (ou Splenda) 500 ml
- 1 tasse noix hachées ou raisins secs (facultatif) 250 ml
- 1 cuillerée à thé bicarbonate de sodium 5 ml
- 1 cuillerée à thé sel 5 ml
- 3 œufs
- 1 cuillerée à thé cannelle 5 ml
- 2 tasses bananes écrasées (env. 5 moyennes) 500 ml
- 1 1/4 tasse ananas broyé non égoutté 398 ml
- 1 tasse huile végétale 250 ml

Directions

1. Dans un grand bol, mélanger la farine, le sucre, les noix, le bicarbonate de sodium, le sel et la cannelle.
2. Dans un autre bol, battre les œufs. Y incorporer les bananes, l'ananas et l'huile. Verser sur les ingrédients secs et mélanger juste pour humidifier.
3. Avec une cuillère répartir la préparation dans de grands moules à muffins graissés (ou avec papier) en les remplissants aux deux tiers.
4. Cuire dans un four préchauffer à 350°F (180°C) pendant 20 à 30 minutes (chaque four étant différent) ou jusqu'à ce que les muffins soient fermes au toucher. Donne 30 muffins.

Recipe submitted by Diane David of Trois Rivières, Quebec, a Navy colleague of Patsy Hennessy, serving together in CFS Shelburne in the 1980s.

annie's oatmeal cookies

Submitted by Maurita Bourque

Ingredients

- 1 cup shortening or margarine
- 1 cup brown sugar
- 2 cups oatmeal
- 1/2 teaspoon salt
- 2 cups flour
- 1/3 cup boiling water and 1 teaspoon soda (mixed together)

Patsy Hennessy, Claudette Downing, Maurita Bourque at the Nepisiquit Archives. Maurita's mother was Annie (Morrissey) Furlotte.

Directions

1. Cream shortening, sugar.
2. Add water, soda alternatively with dry ingredients.
3. Place a small amount on a greased cookie sheet and pat down with a fork.
4. Bake 375°F for 8-10 minutes.

Annie (Morrissey) Furlotte (1904-2000) married Isaac Furlotte in 1933 and spent her entire life in the Jacquet River area. A very accomplished and popular cook, she was known far around for her meals and sweets. Her daughter Maurita Bourque is a very good friend of Patsy Hennessy and together they established the Archives Nepisiquit Archives in 2002. Maurita submitted this recipe in memory of her mother, Annie (Morrissey) Furlotte.

annie's peanut butter cookies

Submitted by Maurita Bourque

Ingredients

- 1 cup shortening
- 1 cup white sugar
- 1 cup brown sugar
- 2 eggs, well beaten
- 1 tsp vanilla
- 1 cup peanut butter
- 3 cups flour
- 1 tsp baking soda
- 1/2 tsp salt

Directions

1. Cream sugar and shortening.
2. Add beaten eggs, peanut butter, vanilla.
3. Sift flour, baking soda and salt.
4. Bake until brown.
5. Bake 350°F for 12 -15 minutes.

Annie (Morrissey) Furlotte with her three little girls in a photo taken in 1941.

Submitted by Maurita Bourque in memory of her mother, Annie (Morrissey) Furlotte.

pickled crab apples

Submitted by Lucy (Hennessy) Jarratt

Ingredients

- 4 quarts crab apples
- 1 tbsp whole cloves
- 2 sticks cinnamon
- 2 cups vinegar
- 5 cups brown sugar
- 1 tbsp allspice

Directions

1. Wash crab apples.
2. Combine remaining ingredients and simmer for 20 minutes.
3. Add apples a few at a time and simmer until tender.
4. Pack apples in hot sterilized jars. Cover with syrup.

Lucy (Hennessy) Jarratt in a photo taken outside the Doucet Hennessy House in 1929, when she was 12 years old.

porcupines

Submitted by Anna (Hennessy) Wesenberg

Ingredients

- 1 tbsp butter
- 1 cup white sugar
- 2 eggs
- 1 cup dates (cut up)
- 1 cup walnuts (cut up)
- 1 tsp vanilla
- 1 dash of salt
- 2 packages of coconut (#1 feathered strip)

Anna (Hennessy) and Henrik Wesenberg on their wedding day, June 1, 1946. This photo was taken on the lawn of the Doucet Hennessy House.

Directions

1. Mix first seven ingredients together.
2. Roll one tsp of mixture into a small balls and roll in coconut until solid.
3. Place in greased cookie sheet.
4. Bake until brown at 350°F.

Anna (Hennessy) Wesenberg was born February 24, 1919, in the Doucet Hennessy House in Bathurst, NB. After graduation she did secretarial work for Bathurst Power & Paper until her marriage to Henrik Aas Wesenberg on June 1, 1946 after which they moved to his home in Oslo, Norway. The couple returned to Bathurst in 1951 to live and raised a family of six children, Jens "Bobby", Halldis, Frederik, Harald, Henrik, and Thomas. Anna is well-known throughout the area for her superb knitting, as well as her excellent cooking.

mom's pumpkin bread

Submitted by Clare (O'Connell) Noon

Ingredients

- 1 cup (250mL) sugar
- 1/2 cup (125mL) oil
- 2 eggs
- 1 cup (250mL) cooked pumpkin
- 1 1/2 cups (375mL) flour
- 1 tsp (5mL) baking powder
- 1 tsp (5mL) baking soda
- 1 tsp (5mL) ground cinnamon
- 1 tsp (5mL) ground nutmeg
- 1/2 tsp (2mL) ground cloves
- 1/2 tsp (2mL) salt
- 3/4 cup (175mL) raisins

Ezella Frenette O'Connell circa 1937 taken in Montreal Photo Studio.

Directions

1. Preheat oven to 350°F (180°C) oven.
2. Grease and flour a loaf pan.
3. Cream the sugar, the oil and the eggs together.
4. Add all of the other ingredients and mix well.
5. Bake in a loaf pan at 350°F for 1 hour (check with toothpick, should come out clean).

This recipe was submitted by Clare (O'Connell) Noon in her mother's memory.

mom's pumpkin marmalade

Submitted by Clare (O'Connell) Noon

Ingredients

- 10 cups peeled, grated pumpkin (1 medium pie pumpkin or half large one)
- 6 oranges, just the juice and zest (makes approx. 3.5 cups juice + 2/3 cup zest)
- 6 lemons, just the juice and zest (makes approx. 2 cups juice + 1/2 cup zest)
- 6 cups sugar

Directions

1. Wash oranges and lemons in hot, soapy water. Rinse well!

Ezella Frenette O'Connell (1913-2000) in LaTuque, Québec.

2. In a thick-bottomed stock pot place the pumpkin, zest, juice and sugar and bring to a boil, and simmer for about 15 minutes. (Mom always did this at night)
3. Remove from heat and allow to cool for an hour or so. Cover and leave in a cool spot overnight.
4. Next morning mix well and simmer, uncovered, on medium heat, for 1 hour until mixture thickens (pumpkin is clear).
5. In other words, cook until a spoonful of the syrup jells firmly on a cool plate, about an hour. The marmalade wrinkles when you push it with your finger after the marmalade has sat for a few minutes on a cold plate in the freezer.
6. Really let the marmalade cool before you put it into jars. 20 minutes of occasional gentle stirring is not too long!
7. Pour into clean sterilized glass jars and seal immediately. Makes about eight 500mL Mason jars or 13 small 250mL jars.

This recipe was submitted by Clare (O'Connell) Noon in her mother's memory.

momma's shortcake

Submitted by Lucy (Hennessy) Jarratt

Ingredients

- 2 cups flour
- 1/2 cup shortening
- 4 tsp baking powder
- 1/2 tsp Salt
- 1 large egg
- 1 cup milk

Sidney and Lucy (Hennessy) Jarratt on their wedding day, August 26, 1942. This photo was taken in front of the Doucet Hennessy House.

Directions

1. Mix flour, shortening, baking powder, and salt together.
2. Add the egg and milk and mix well.
3. Knead until smooth.
4. Roll out to 1/2 inch.
5. Cut with large cookie cutter.
6. Flour the cutting board so batter won't stick.
7. Bake at 400°F for 12-14 minutes.

eileen's scotch cookies

Submitted by Lucy (Hennessy) Jarratt

Ingredients

- 1 cup butter
- 2 cups flour
- 5 tbsp icing sugar (sifted)

Directions

1. Cream butter very well.
2. Slowly add icing sugar and flour.
3. Mix by hand until everything is well mixed.
4. Pat out to 1/2 inch thick.
5. Cut out with small cutter.
6. Bake 10-12 minutes at 325°F.

Roger and Eileen (O'Toole) Hennessy on their wedding day July 30, 1940. This photo was taken outside the Doucet Hennessy House.

Eileen Frances O'Toole Hennessy (1919-2006) was born in Sout h Nelson in the Miramichi and moved with her family to Bat hurst at age eight. She loved to golf and act in local plays where she met Roger Hennessy, whom she married in 1940. The couple raised five children; Patsy, Sharon, Anna, Jimmy and Tommy. Eileen was famous around the Village for her chicken bouillon and mouth- watering scotch cookies.

soft molasses cookies

Submitted by Lorraine (Christie) Doucet

Ingredients

- 1 1/3 cups shortening
- 1 cup white sugar
- 2 eggs
- 1 1/3 cups molasses
- 1/2 cup cold water
- 4 tsp baking soda
- 1/2 tsp salt
- 1 tsp ground cloves
- 1 tsp cinnamon
- 4 cups flour (or more)

Lorraine (Christie) Doucet and Lucy (Hennessy) Jarratt hold their granddaughters, Payton and Kersten, Easter 2011.

Directions

1. Cream shortening and sugar together.
2. Add unbeaten eggs.
3. Add molasses.
4. Dissolve soda and salt in a little hot water and add the cold water.
5. Sift flour and spices together.
6. Roll and bake in hot oven 375°F for 10-12 minutes.

Lorraine (Christie) Doucet was born on September 3, 1935, the daughter of William and Adeline (Chiasson) Christie. She married Ralph Doucet, the son of Frank P. and Anne (Mazzerole) Doucet. They had four children, Anne Marie, Robert, Bev and Sandra.

papa's strawberry shortcake

Submitted by Patricia Hennessy

Ingredients

- 4 cups flour
- 7 tsp baking powder
- 2 tbsp sugar
- 1 tsp salt
- 1 cup shortening
- 2 eggs
- 1 cup milk (allow less milk for extra egg, recipe calls for 1 egg)

Patrick Hennessy and his daughter Anna in a photo taken on December 9, 1940 in the front yard of the Doucet Hennessy House.

Directions

1. Mix together then cut in 2 pieces.
2. Roll each piece 1/2 inch thick. Place 1 in pan and butter the top. Place other piece on top of that.
3. For individual buns, roll and cut out with cookie cutter or drinking glass.
4. Bake at 375°F for 25-30 minutes or at 400°F for individual buns for 15 minutes.
5. After the large one is cooked, separate the two layers carefully, put strawberries in between and replace the top layer over the berries.
6. Cover each portion with whipped cream.

maman's sugar cookies

Submitted by Carol Doucet

Ingredients

- 3/4 cup margarine or butter
- 1 egg
- 1 cup sugar
- 4 teaspoons evaporated milk
- 2 teaspoons imitation vanilla
- 2 1/2 cups all purpose flour
- 2 1/2 teaspoons baking powder

Drawing of woman gathering wood, by Carol Doucet.

Directions

1. Take sugar, egg and margarine and beat well.
2. Take flour and baking powder and stir together.
3. Mix all ingredients well and when well done, take a little round ball and roll it well; drop in pan.
4. Press with fork lengthwise and crosswise. Sprinkle with sugar before baking. Bake in greased pan at 375°F for 6 to 8 minutes until edges are golden brown.
5. P.S. - You can make cookies plain or add chocolate chips, pecans, coconut, raisins, or peanut butter before baking.
6. To make another interesting design on cookie before baking, press one end of an empty thread spool into margarine and sugar and press into top of each cookie.

This was a recipe passed on to us by my mother. She was an avid baker and sometimes baked cookies, pies, cakes, home-made bread on almost a daily basis. We have fond memories of her and the grandchildren (both boys and girls) hard at work around the kitchen table creating these delicious treats. As the children grew older they got more creative and designed angels, wreaths, hearts, and other shapes (all freehand and without a cookie cutter.) Then came the best part - sharing these delicious cookies, accompanied by a glass of cold milk, with family. Carol Doucet is the Vice- President of LLDM (Les Doucet Du Monde) - Doucets of the World and he lives in Lafayette, Louisiana.

papa's tea biscuits

Submitted by Patsy Hennessy

Ingredients

- 2 cups flour
- 1/4 cup margarine
- 1/2 tsp salt
- 1 cup milk
- 4 tsp baking powder
- 1 tbsp Sugar

Directions

1. Mix together. Roll out about 1/4 inch thick.
2. Cut individual biscuits with cookie cutter, or water glass.
3. Bake 400°F for 10-12 minutes.

Beatrice and Patrick Hennessy and Francis "Fanny" Hennessy in a photo taken outside the Doucet Hennessy House in 1945.

thimble cakes

Submitted by Lucy (Hennessy) Jarratt

Ingredients

- 1/2 cup butter
- 1/4 cup sugar
- 1 egg yolk
- 1 cup flour

Directions

1. Mix and add 1 tsp vanilla.
2. Roll in small ball.
3. Dip in unbeaten egg white.
4. Roll in finely chopped walnuts
5. Dent with a thimble. Cook for 5 minutes at 350°F and dent again.
6. Cook until brown.
7. Fill center with jelly.

Jarratt children; Sally (running), Billy (standing), and Anne (sitting) in a photo taken on the lawn of the Doucet Hennessy House 1948.

homemade yogurt

Submitted by Melynda Jarratt

Ingredients

Jarratt family photo, taken 1964.
Melynda is at bottom right.

- Milk or soy milk *
- Plain yogurt
- Yogurt machine (There are all kinds of yogurt machines on the market. I use a 5 cup Salton yogurt machine, which acts like an "incubator" to keep the five individual yogurt cups warm over an 8 hour period, but you can make yogurt in a thermos, an oven, on a heating pad, in the sun, on a wood stove, and in a crockpot. The goal is to keep the bacteria growing in a warm environment.
- * Alternatively, to make low fat yogurt use low fat milk, no fat soy milk and low fat or no fat yogurt.

Directions

1. Using the Saltone yogurt cups as a measure, pour five yogurt cups of milk / soy milk into a pot on the stove and bring to a boil, carefully stirring to avoid burning the milk on the bottom of the pot. If it burns, use a strainer to remove the burnt milk.
2. When the milk reaches a boil, turn off the heat and let the milk cool down until it is no longer burning hot. If you can put your finger in the milk for ten seconds and it doesn't burn, it's time to put the yogurt into the warm milk.
3. Put a half cup of yogurt or more as you wish into the warm milk stirring until the yogurt is dissolved.
4. Pour the milk / yogurt mixture into the cups, cover and let the yogurt machine do its magic. In about 8 hours you will have your own homemade yogurt.
5. Add berries or fruit to make a healthy, light snack.
6. There are all kinds of yogurt recipes on the internet so give it try! You'll be surprised how inexpensive and easy it is to make.

Melynda Jarratt is the grand- daughter of Patrick and Beatrice Hennessy. Born in 1961, she was only member of the Jarratt family who did not grow up in the Doucet Hennessy House; however she has many fond memories of the house, her grandparents, her Aunt Anna and Uncle Henrik Wesenberg, as well as 27 Wesenberg and Hennessy first cousins. Melynda is a founding Board Member of the AMDHHA Inc.

Hennessy children, left to right: Roger, Manus, Lucy and Anna (sitting) in a studio portrait taken about 1920. Five more children would follow - James, Dorothy, Varrily, Bruno and Robert. Photo from the Hennessy Fonds, PANB.

sauces, soups, chowders & main dishes

. . .

Sauces, soupes, chaudrées et plats principaux

Recipes appear in the language they were submitted.
Les recettes paraissent dans la langue dans laquelle elles ont été soumises.

terri's bbq sauce

Submitted by Terri Jarratt

Ingredients

- 1 cup of brown sugar
- 1 cup of water stir together
- 1/2 cup of white vinegar
- 1 tsp A1 or sweet chili sauce
- 1/2 cup of catsup

Directions

Terri Jarratt, Easter, 2011.

1. Mix all ingredients together then add a teaspoon of either A1 sauce or sweet chili sauce.
2. Best with pork ribs that have been boiled for 1 hour and 1/2. Pour sauce over ribs, put in oven at 350°F for 20 minutes, then baste the ribs, turn up stove to 400°F for 20 more minutes. Then serve them up.

Terri Jarratt is the granddaughter of Patrick and Beatrice Hennessy. She teaches in Bathurst at the Transition Centre where she specializes in Methods and Resources. Terri spent the first three years of her life in the Doucet Hennessy House before the Jarratt family moved to their own house at the top of what is now Hennessy Street in Hennessy Subdivision.

boston baked beans

Submitted by David MacLeod

Ingredients

Thomas and Moise Jean Doucet, of Cheticamp and Grand Etang, Nova Scotia.

- 1 pound of beans - Navy, Northern, Jacobs Cattle or other small dried bean.
- 3 strips of uncooked bacon, cut in thirds. (1/4 pound of salt pork is an alternate).
- 1 onion, finely diced
- 2 tbsp molasses
- 2 tsp salt
- 1/4 tsp ground black pepper
- 1/4 tsp of thyme
- 1/8 tsp of ground cloves
- 1/4 tsp dry mustard
- 1 tsp Dijon Mustard (optional)
- 1/2 cup ketchup
- 1 tbsp Worcestershire sauce
- 1/8 cup brown sugar

Directions

1. Soak beans overnight or longer in cold water. Simmer the beans in the same water until tender and the skins will blow open - approximately 1 to 2 hours. Drain and reserve the liquid.
2. Preheat oven to 325°F (165°C).
3. Arrange the beans in a 2 quart bean pot or casserole dish by placing a portion of the beans in the bottom of dish, and layering them with bacon strip pieces and onion. Note, if salt pork is used instead of the bacon, cut through the rind to a depth of 1/2 inch and place the pork on top of the beans.
4. In a saucepan, combine some reserved liquid with the molasses, salt, pepper, dry mustard, thyme, cloves, ketchup, Worcestershire sauce and brown sugar. Bring the mixture to a boil and pour over beans. Pour in just enough of the reserved bean water to cover the beans. Cover the dish with a lid or aluminum foil.

5. Bake for 3-4 hours in the preheated oven, until beans are tender. Remove the lid about halfway through cooking. Add more liquid from the reserve if necessary to prevent the beans from getting too dry. Just keep them barely covered with the reserved liquid throughout the cooking process. Enjoy!

What other recipe to choose for our grandfather than the renowned staple, Boston Baked Beans. It would have been more simply prepared in their day and likely only composed of beans, salt pork, molasses, onion, mustard, salt and pepper. Soak up the juices with your choice of brown or cornbread. Dave MacLeod is a member of Les Doucet du Monde and lives in Scarborough, Maine, USA.

Thomas F. Doucet (left) and his brother, Moise Jean. Moise was the first Acadian elected to the Nova Scotia Legislature in the late 1800s. The brothers grew up in Cheticamp and Grand Etang. Thomas is the grandfather of Dave MacLeod, who is a member of Les Doucet du Monde (LDDM) - Doucets of the World. Photo courtesy of Dave MacLeod.

fanny's cabbage rolls

Submitted by Frances (Garrett) Hennessy

Ingredients

- 2 Lbs Extra Lean Hamburger
- 1 cup white rice (uncooked)
- 1 green pepper
- 1 litre ketchup
- 1 large cabbage
- 1 large onion
- 1 large V-8 Juice (original)
- 2 eggs
- Roasting pan
- Medium Ziplock freezer bags

A war time photo of James and Frances (Garrett) Hennessy taken in the front yard of t he Doucet Hennessy House (Holy Family Church is in background).

Directions

1. Chop green pepper & onion into small pieces. Put them into a mixing bowl with hamburger, raw rice, eggs, and 2 cups of ketchup. Mix well. Add a tablespoon of salt and 1-2 teaspoons of pepper.
2. Cut out the core of the cabbage. Put cabbage in boiling water up to about half way on cabbage. Cook for 5 minutes then turn cabbage upside down in boiling water and cook 5 minutes.
3. Remove cabbage carefully so you don't ruin the leaves. Set on board and remove leaves by peeling off. When you get to those not easy to just peel off, put cabbage back in boiling water for a bit as before to soften more leaves.
4. For large cabbage leaves, cut the spine out, thus making two. Put in meat mixture and roll.
5. Using a roasting pan, pour in one can of tomato soup and its equivalent amount of water just as though you were going to heat it as soup. Lay all the filled cabbage rolls out in the pan.
6. Pour the second can of tomato soup and water over them. Pour the V-8 juice over as well. Pour the rest of the ketchup over it all. Sprinkle the salt and pepper on top.

7. Cover the pan with either tin foil or a cover that belongs to the pan. Bake in oven for 1 1/2 hours at 350°F.

James "Bunny" and Frances "Fanny" Hennessy had two children: Patrick and Nancy. This recipe is what has made Fanny one of the Hennessy family's favourite cooks. Her son-in- law Bill Lynch even gave her a trophy attesting to her being the world's best cabbage roll maker.

cabbage soup

Submitted by Thérèse E. (Comeau) Hennessy

Ingredients

- 1 head of cabbage
- 6 green onions
- 2 green peppers
- 1 bunch of celery
- 1 can diced tomatoes
- 2 cans tomato soup
- 1 can tomato paste
- Salt and pepper to taste

Thérèse E. (Comeau) Hennessy, left, as a young woman during her nurse's training in Bathurst.

Optional Ingredients

- 1 cauliflower
- 6 diced potatoes
- 1 bunch of carrots
- 1 turnip

Directions

1. Chop 1 head of cabbage, 6 green onions, 2 green peppers, 1 bunch of celery.
2. Place in soup pot.
3. Add 1 can of diced tomatoes, 2 cans of tomato soup and 1 can of tomato paste.
4. Add enough water to cover.
5. Season with salt and pepper.
6. Bring to a boil, reduce heat, and simmer until veggies are tender.

casserole au chou

Soumis par Francine (Doucet) Daigle

Ingredients

- 1 gros chou coupé en gros morceaux
- 2 c. à T de beurre
- 3 à 4 c. à T de farine
- Lait ou eau
- Un peu de chapelure
- Un peu du fromage.

Jackie Auclair, Francine (Doucet) Daigle et sa soeur Andréa Doucet. Ste.-Louise, N.-B., 2009.

Directions

1. Faire cuire dans l'eau 1 gros chou coupé en gros morceaux.
2. Enlever l'eau complètement et placer le chou dans une casserole 9 X 13.
3. Faire une sauce béchamel.
4. Lait ou eau en brassant constamment. Assaisonner au goût.
5. Vider sur le chou.
6. Ajouter un peu de chapelure et du fromage.
7. Faire fondre le fromage au four et servir.

Recette de Rita Doucet soumise par sa fille Francine (Doucet) Daigle. Francine a apporté cette casserole au souper à la fortune du pot, levée de fonds pour la Maison Doucet Hennessy à l'été 2011. Elle l'a aussi servie au souper de la Famille Doucet en l'honneur des LDDM (Les Doucet du monde) à Robertville durant le CMA 2009, à la maison où elle a grandi. / Francine (Doucet) Daigle brought this recipe to the Doucet Hennessy fundraiser pot luck in the summer of 2011. She also served it at the Doucet family supper we had for the LDDM (The Doucets of the World) in Robertville during CMA (World Acadian Congress) 2009, at the house where she grew up.

chaudrée de palourdes

Soumis par Marie (Doucet) Boulay

Ingrédients

Le comité organisateur de la
Rencontre des Doucet au
CONGRÈS MONDIAL ACADIEN
2009.

- 30 ml (2 c à soupe) de beurre
- 1/2 tasses (125 ml) d'oignon coupé en dés
- 1 tasse (250 ml) d'eau chaude
- 1 tasse (250 ml) de pommes de terre crues, en dés
- 1/2 tasse (125 ml) de céleri, en dés
- 10 oz. (284 ml) de palourdes et leur jus
- 2 tasses (500 ml) de lait
- 1/2 cuillerée à thé (2.5 ml) de poivre
- 1 cuillerée à thé (5 ml) de sel

Directions

1. Dans une casserole, faire fondre le beurre et revenir les oignons et le céleri.
2. Ajouter l'eau et les pommes de terre et cuire jusqu'à tendreté.
3. Ajouter les palourdes et leur jus, le lait, le sel et le poivre.
4. Laisser mijoter à feu doux de 20 à 25 minutes.

Lors du CONGRÈS MONDIAL ACADIEN 2009, le comité organisateur de la RENCONTRE DE LA FAMILLE DOUCET, tous des petits-enfants à Jos à Tanis (Robertville) à Dosit hée (Petit- Rocher) ont reçu les représentants des Doucet du Monde à un pot luck géant à la maison construite par Dosit hée dans les années 1880, propriété actuelle de Véronique Doucet , fille de Gérard à Armand à Jos à Tanis à Dosit hée. La maison, la cour et le perron étaient remplis de Doucet!! Nous, les Doucet de la famille de Jos à Tanis Doucet de Ste- Louise de Robertville et les Doucet de LDDM, tous des États-Unis, avons vécu une soirée mémorable. La fête s'est continuée le lendemain et le surlendemain à Grande-Anse. Notre Rencontre de la grande famille Doucet a été un succès.

chili

Submitted by Sister Aurea Cormier

Ingredients

Sister Aurea Cormier, November, 2011.

- 454g (1 lb.) Red Kidney Beans (Thomson's sells red Kidney beans)
- 4 cups cold water
- 1 lb. lean ground beef
- 2 medium onions chopped
- 2 stalks celery, chopped
- 2 cloves garlic, minced
- 1 green pepper, chopped
- 1 (540 ml) can tomatoes
- 1 tbsp chili powder
- 2 tsp cocoa powder
- 2 tsp ground cumin
- 1 tsp salt
- 1/4 tsp chili pepper flakes
- 1/4 tsp. cinnamon
- 1 (398 ml) can tomato sauce

Directions

1. Sort and rinse beans. Soak beans overnight in cold water. Drain.
2. Add 4 cups cold water, cover, heat to boiling, simmer 50 minutes or until nearly tender. Drain.
3. Cook ground beef in large skillet until brown, then add onions, celery, garlic and green pepper. Cook for 15 minutes or until onion is clear.
4. Stir in tomatoes, breaking up with fork, chili powder, cocoa, salt, chili flakes and cinnamon. Cook for 5 minutes. Stir in kidney beans and tomato sauce.
5. For a vegetarian alternative, omit ground beef. Add 1 can (199 ml) kernel corn when adding tomato sauce.

Sister Aurea Cormier is a nutritionist, social activist and member of the Order of New Brunswick. She volunteers with Melynda Jarratt and many other New Brunswickers in the NB Common Front for Social Justice. Recipe developed by the Ontario Coloured Bean Grower Association.

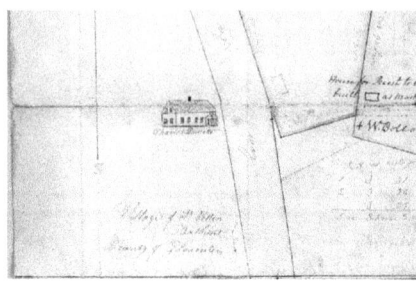

Middle right: An image of the Charles Doucette House as it appeared on the 1837 Kings Survey. Photo courtesy of PANB. *Bottom left:* The new logo of the Doucet Hennessy House, designed by Meghan Coates of Fredericton, NB.

A drawing of the Doucet Hennessy House in the 20th century.

The 2011 logo of the Doucet Hennessy House, designed by Meghan Coates of Fredericton, NB.

chow

Submitted by Thérèse (Comeau) Hennessy

Ingredients

Hennessy, Wesenberg and Jarratt parents and children gather for a photo outside the front entrance to the Doucet Hennessy House. Dr. Robert Hennessy is sitting on the steps, top left, and Thérèse is sitting, far right, in polka dot dress, May 1958.

- 15 pounds of tomatoes (green)
- 5 pounds of onions (white)
- 5 pounds of white sugar
- 2 tablespoons pickling spices (put in bag)
- 1/2 gallon of vinegar (8 cups or 2 liters)
- 3/4 cup coarse salt (to be discarded after use)

Directions

1. The evening before, cut up tomatoes and onions in thin slices (like onion rings) and place in a large cooking pot.
2. Add 3/4 cup of coarse salt and then fill with water so that it covers all the tomatoes and onions. Soak overnight.
3. In morning, drain brine (salt water) and add 5 pounds of white sugar, 1/2 gallon of vinegar and pickling spice in a bag.
4. Cook slowly for 2 1/4 hours over low – medium temperature. Stir frequently. Makes approximately 20 bottles.

cipâte

Submitted by Rolande Doucet O'Connell

Pastry Ingredients

Jos (1886-1969) et Gilbert Doucet
(1912-1995).

- 4 cups all-purpose flour
- 6 tsp baking powder
- 2 tsp salt
- 1 1/4 cups cold shortening
- Cold milk

Filling Ingredients

- 2 lbs boneless pork (with fat)
- 2 lbs veal (any inexpensive cut)
- 1 1/2 lbs stewing beef
- 2 to 3 lbs fresh chicken, partridge or rabbit
- 3 large onions, chopped fine
- 4 stalks celery, chopped fine
- 2 scraped carrots, thinly sliced
- 1tsp each, nutmeg and rosemary
- 1/2 tsp cinnamon
- 3 or 4 whole cloves
- 1 bay leaf
- 2 tsp each, savory and pepper
- 5 tsp salt
- 1 1/2 cups each, dry white wine and boiling water

Pastry Directions

1. Sift first three ingredients together; cut in shortening until about the size of peas.
2. Stir in just enough cold milk to make a stiff dough.
3. Form into a ball and chill in refrigerator while preparing meat.

Filling Directions

1. Have ready 1 deep 5-quart, or a pair of 2 1/2-quart covered casseroles. (Cast-iron or cast aluminum Dutch ovens may also be successfully used.)
2. Cut fat off pork in small dice and sprinkle over bottom of pot. Cut remaining pork, veal, beef and chicken into inch cubes and mix together. (Save skin and bones of the chicken for soup stock later.)
3. Combine all vegetables, herbs and seasonings, but exclude liquids.
4. Place a third of the mixed meat over the pork fat; top with a third of the vegetable mixture.
5. Now roll out a third of the pastry to fit the pot and cover vegetable-meat arrangement. Gash pastry with 3 or 4 openings.
6. Repeat layers in the same order, finally covering with remaining third of pastry. Trim. Cut neat openings in top. Decorate edge with a twist of braid rolled pastry scraps.
7. It is best to prepare the pie up to this point 2 or 3 hours before cooking or the day before. Refrigerate until cooking time.
8. Just before baking, pour a mixture of wine and water slowly through the top pastry openings. If mixture seems firmly packed, lift the edges with a fork until all liquids runs to bottom of dish.
9. Cover airtight and bake at 300°F for 4 or 5 hours.
10. After 2 hours cooking, add a small quantity of boiling water if pie filling seems dry.
11. Present as hot main course with vegetables, or refrigerate after cooling and serve as the centre of supper buffet, accompanied with salads and relish.

Rolande Doucet O'Connell est issue d'une des familles nombreuses de Doucet, où la bouffe, qu'elle soit fine ou qu'elle soit grosse, a toujours occupé une place importante dans leur vie quotidienne.

Lorsque Rolande est tombée sur cette recette en 1968, l'année après son mariage, elle l'a vite adoptée comme la sienne. Depuis, elle la concocte au moins une fois par année surtout dans le temps des Fêtes, entre Noël et le Jour de l'An.

Son père Gilbert disait souvent: «On est une terrible de gang pour manger». Elle soumet donc cette recette au nom de Gilbert et celui de son père Jos (à Tanis à Dosithée, à Sylvain à Michel à Charles, né à Népisiguit!!); deux gars natifs de Robertville qui aimaient bien bouffer.

codfish cakes

Submitted by Patsy Hennessy

Ingredients

- 1 lb salted codfish
- 6 medium potatoes
- 6 oz piece of salted pork (bean pork of old)
- 1 medium onion
- 1 egg (optional)
- 1 cup flour (or what is needed)

Patsy Hennessy in her navy uniform, 1969.

Directions

1. Set codfish in large pot of cold water, put on medium heat until simmer starts.
2. Drain fish, rinse a bit with cold water then refill pot with more cold water and repeat above.
3. Do this once more and the fish should then still be salty but not too much.
4. Peel the potatoes and cook as usual. When done, mash them good and let cool.
5. Cut up the salted pork in narrow strips, leaving on the rind. Then score each strip down to the rind about an 8th of an inch apart. Put in cast iron pan on low heat to render the fat from the strips. Don't let smoke or get too hot or it will evaporate. You want the liquid fat for frying the fishcakes later.
6. When the strips are shrivelled up and crispy, remove them, cool, and cut off the scores of fat, put them aside and throw away the rind. Some people like to chew on the rind and that is okay too.
7. Dice the onion up fine then mix them in with the bits of crispy fat.
8. Take a bit of the rendered fat in a smaller pan and fry the onion and bits of fat together fairly hot to brown the onion.
9. Mix the onion and bits of fat into the mashed potatoes well. Should do by hand. Making sure the codfish is broken into little bits, mix in as well. I usually add an egg to hold it all together.
10. Put some flour in a plate for the cakes.

11. Make a ball of the potato, fish mix, about the size of your fist. Flatten it out on wax paper to about 1/2 inch thick. Press into the flour so it is coated on both sides. Repeat until all the mix is made into cakes.

12. In a large iron frying pan put a couple of spoonfuls of the rendered fat and when the fat is good and hot, not burning, lay the cakes in to cook. Let cook on one side until brown and crispy then turn over to do the other side.

13. Put more rendered fat as you need it, remembering to let it get hot again before putting in more cakes.

14. Garnish with chow-chow for really good experience.

Roger and Eileen (O'Toole) Hennessy on their wedding day July 30, 1940. This photo was taken outside the Doucet Hennessy House.

des tailles

Soumis par Jeannine (Doucet) Caissie

Ingrédients

- 3 ou 4 grosses patates, plummées, et coupées en ronds environ 1/4" d'épaisseur.
- 1 ou 2 gros onions blancs ou jaunes, coupes en morceaux.
- Sel et poivre

Jeannine (Doucet) Caissie.

Directions

1. Faire rechauffer une grosse poele de potain sur le feu en ajoutant de la graisse (shortening) et faire ca fondre comme il faut.
2. Une fois que la poele et la graisse sont suffisant chauds, ajouter les onions et les "tailles" de patates, gardant la chaleur assez, sans bruler.
3. A mesure que les onions et les patates deviennent brunes, melanger et tourner les tailles de patates afin qu'elles soient brunes chaque cote, et melanger les onions aussi afin qu'ils soient toutes cuits.
4. Aussitot que les patates sont "grillees" les deux cotes, elles devraient etre cuites, alors je les enleve de la poele et les place sur un "paper-towel" pour les secher de graisse.
5. Les "tailles" sont bonnes servies avec n'importe quoi d'autre types de viande et des legumes, avec du ketchup!

Je n'oserais pas deviner combien de calories il y a dans cette recette, mais c'est tres bon a manger le soir au souper quand il fait froid dehors! Jeannine (Doucet) Caissie. Jeannine est originaire du N.-B., de la région de Moncton.

Elle est déménagée aux Ètats-Unis plus de 50 ans passés, mais elle a gardé son acadienneté. Elle faisait partie de la délégation LDDM (Les Doucet du monde) lors du CMA 2009. / Jeannine is originally from NB, Moncton region. She moved to the United States more than 50 years ago but visits her relatives regularly in Acadie and has retained her Acadian heritage. She was at the CMA (Acadian World Congress) in 2009 along with the LDDM delegation.

papa's dough boys

Submitted by Lucy (Hennessy) Jarratt

Ingredients

- 1 cup of flour
- 2 tsp of baking powder
- Water or milk

Directions

1. Mix the dry ingredients and pour in enough water or milk to make a thick dough.
2. Drop a large spoonful on the top of a stew, cover and cook for ten minutes.
3. Makes a great addition to a beef or chicken stew and is perfect filler for those cold winter nights when there are lots of friends and family around the table.

Patrick Hennessy and cookees, 15 COY, CFC, near Beauly, Scotland.

dumplings

Submitted by Thérèse (Comeau) Hennessy

Ingredients

- 1 cup of flour
- 1/2 tsp salt
- 1 1/2 tsp baking powder
- 1/2 cup of milk
- 2 tbsp melted fat or salad oil

Directions

1. Stir together.
2. Drop spoonfuls over stew.
3. Cover and cook for 15 minutes.

Thérèse E. (Comeau) and Dr. Robert D. Hennessy on their wedding day, June 4, 1955, at Holy Family Church, Bathurst, NB.

fricot typiquement acadien

Soumis par Marie (Doucet) Boulay

Ingrédients

Délégation de Les Doucet du Monde (LDDM) Congrès Mondial Acadien 2009: 1ère rangée, de gauche à droite: Elenora Turnage, Jacqueline Doucet Auclair, Linda Doucette, Edith Doucet Raun, Eldine Doucet, Carol Doucet, Jeannine Doucet Caissie, Paul Caissie. Deuxième rangée: Gary Auclair, Norman Doucette, William Raun.

- 2 litres d'eau
- 1 1/2 livre de pilons de poulet
- 4 cuillerées à soupe de margarine
- 1 oignon
- 6 carottes moyennes coupées en rondelles
- 10 patates moyennes
- 2 cuillerées à thé de sel
- 1 cuillerée à thé de poivre
- 2 tasses de farine
- 2 cuillerées à table de poudre magique
- 2 cuillerées à table de bouillon de poulet
- 1 cuillerée à table de sarriette

Directions

1. Faire bouillir l'eau avec la margarine et l'oignon.
2. Ajouter les pilons de poulet, 1 c. à thé de sel et de poivre.
3. Faire mijoter pendant 20 minutes à feu moyen.
4. Ajouter les carottes et laisser mijoter 10 minutes.
5. Ajouter les patates, le bouillon de poulet et la sarriette.
6. Faire mijoter 20 minutes ou jusqu'à ce que les patates soient cuites.
7. Dans un bol, mettre la farine, la poudre magique et une c. à thé de sel.
8. Mélanger bien le tout.
9. Ajouter du bouillon qui bouille pour faire une pâte assez épaisse (comme une abaisse à tarte).
10. Rajouter dans le fricot en faisant des boules d'environ 2 pouces de diamètre. Laisser mijoter avec le couvercle environs 5 minutes.

everyday meatloaf

Submitted by Thérèse E. (Comeau) Hennessy

Ingredients

- 2/3 cup dry bread crumbs
- 1 cup of milk
- 1 1/2 lb of ground beef
- 2 beaten eggs
- 1/4 cup grated onions
- 1 tsp salt
- 1/2 tsp garlic pepper
- 1/2 tsp sage

Piquant Sauce Ingredients

- 3 tbsp of brown sugar
- 1/4 cup of ketchup
- 1/4 tsp of nutmeg
- 1 tsp of dry mustard

Dr. Robert (Bobby) and Thérèse E. (Comeau) Hennessy on their 25th wedding anniversary in 1980.

Directions

1. Soak bread crumbs in milk, add eggs, meat, onions, and seasoning.
2. Mix well and cover.
3. Make Piquant Sauce.
4. Cover the meatloaf mixture with piquant sauce and bake at 350 degrees Fahrenheit for 1 hour.

moose meat stew for ten

Submitted by Gilbert Sewell

Ingredients

- 3 pounds moose meat (cut up in small pieces)
- Salt
- Pepper
- Onion (large) - chopped
- 5 pounds medium potatoes - chopped
- 2 pounds carrots - chopped
- 1 medium turnip
- 4 cubes - OXO
- Cornstarch

Gilbert Sewell at the Doucet Hennessy booth in the Bathurst Farmers Market.

Directions

1. Use a large pot to simmer the meat with salt, pepper, onion, OXO cubes, 4- 6 cups of water, and cook for about 2 hours.
2. Add the cut up vegetables, potatoes and simmer for about 1 hour.
3. Option: to thicken stew, mix 1/2 cup of water and 2 tbsp of cornstarch and slowly stir into stew.

Gilbert Sewell is a Mi'kmaq elder, historian, folklorist, storyteller, guide, wood-carver, and Mi'kmaq language instructor from Pabineau First Nation.

oven stew in red wine

Submitted by Rolande Doucet O'Connell

Ingredients

- 2 pounds beef chuck, cut in cubes
- 2 medium onions, sliced
- 2 cloves of garlic, crushed
- 3 tablespoons flour
- 2 teaspoon salt
- ¼ teaspoon pepper
- ½ teaspoon thyme
- 1 small bay leaf, crumbled
- 1 teaspoon bottled gravy browning
- 1 can (10 oz.) Mushrooms
- 1 can (14 oz.) Tomato sauce
- 1 can (10 oz.) Beef bouillon
- 1 cup red wine
- Chopped parsley for garnish

*Rolande Doucet O'Connell
December,1973. Bathurst, NB.*

Directions

1. In Dutch oven or heavy casserole, mix all ingredients except liquids.
2. Stir in liquids. Cover and bake in 350° F oven for three hours or until meat is very tender, stirring occasionally.
3. Taste and adjust seasoning.
4. Sprinkle with chopped parsley and serve right from the casserole into bowls.
5. Accompany with red wine, a big tossed green salad, and lots of crusty French breads for dipping in the sauce. Serve 4 to 6.
6. Enjoy!

Notes

- Cubed raw potatoes may be added during the last hour.
- Note from Rolande: I also add big chunks of carrots before I stir in the liquids.

This recipe tastes much better if you bake it in a cast iron pot. I have cooked this stew several times a year for over thirty 30 years. It is always popular at a potluck. I brought it to the Doucet Hennessy House Potluck fundraiser in Beresford, this past summer.

Ce ragoût est beaucoup plus savoureux lorsqu'on le cuit dans une marmite en fonte. Je l'ai concocté maintes fois au courant des dernières trente années. Il est toujours un succès dans les soupers à la fortune du pot. Je l'ai servi au Souper levée de fond de La Maison Doucet Hennessy, à Beresford l'été passé.

Rolande Doucet O'Connell est une infirmière à la retraite, mariée à Rod O'Connell. Elle est née à Sormany , et vit à Trembla y N-B. Elle est mère de trois enfants et de trois petites-filles. Ses passe-temps préférés depuis sa retraite sont les voyages, la lecture, le jardinage, et les journées à la plage l'été avec sa famille. / Rolande is a retired nurse, married to Rod O'Connell. She was born in Sormany NB, and now lives in Trembla y, NB. She is the mother of three children and three grand-daughters. Her main pastimes since retirement include travelling, reading, flower gardening, and enjoying the beach at their cottage in Beresford with her family in the summer.

Bas au milieu: Apollinaire et Marie-Anne (Cormier) Frenette dans une photo prise vers 1950. Ils sont les grands-parents de Rod O'Connell, dont l'épouse, Rolande Doucet O'Connell, est la co-présidente fondatrice de l'Association Maison Doucet Hennessy House Association Inc. Photo gracieuseté de Clare O'Connell Noon.

grandma's pâtés

Submitted by Thérèse E. (Comeau) Hennessy

Meat Filling Ingredients

- 5 lbs. boneless stew beef
- 3 lbs. fresh lean pork
- 1/2 lb. fresh pork fat
- 2 medium onions

50th anniversary of Patrick and Beatrice Hennessy's wedding in 1961. Thérèse at bottom right.

Pastry Ingredients

- 2 cups flour
- 1/2 tsp salt
- 2 tsp. baking powder
- 6 tbsp water
- 1 cup shortening

Directions

1. Cook and keep meat separately. Take meat out of water when cooked.
2. Cover beef with water and 1 tbsp salt, less salt for other meats. Boil slowly for 2 1/2 hours. Save this water for gravy.
3. Keep 3 pieces of pork and fat to put with beef after 1/2 hour of hour of boiling.
4. Cook pork, also fat, with about 2 hours with tbsp. salt in each.
5. Prepare all meats separately and into a large dish.
6. Pass all meats through chopper, alternating beef and pork and pieces of cut onions.
7. Make gravy, adding a pinch of pepper and leave to cool a little, then add all meats and mix gently, saving a small quantity of gravy in case you may need some to add later.
8. Take a small amount of pastry at a time and roll on floured board, cutting into squares about 4-5 inches and put meat in centre.
9. Fold over pastry and press edges.
10. Brush with milk just before placing in the oven.

11. Bake at 400'F for 30 minutes.
12. To reheat, put in very low heat oven for 1 hour. If desired, make as ordinary pies.
13. Meat substitutes: left over roast, steak and a little fat, also some hamburg lightly cooked in shortening.

Thérèse E. (Comeau) Hennessy is the daughter of Charles Comeau and Marguerite Melanson. She grew up in Bathurst Village and trained as a registered nurse. She married Robert D. Hennessy, MD in 1955 and the couple raised six children, Barbara, Colleen, Shawn, Carol, Timothy and Michael. Thérèse and her family lived next to the Doucet Hennessy House for the last forty years and for many years Christmas Eve was the occasion of open house for extended family in their home with Thérèse making some wonderful treats, two of which are her mouth-watering meat pies and chow.

Thérèse E. (Comeau) and Dr. Robert D. Hennessy on their wedding day, June 4, 1955, at Holy Family Church, Bathurst, NB.

scallop & lobster casserole

Submitted by Elmyra Lloyd

Main Ingredients

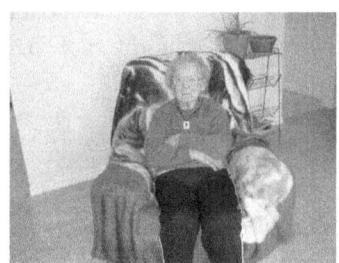

- 1/2 lb scallops
- 1 lb lobster
- 1 cup white rice
- 2 hard boiled eggs
- 1 cup green/red peppers
- 1/2 lb fresh mushrooms
- 1 tbsp butter
- 1 can mushroom soup

Elmyra Lloyd in a recent photo, November, 2011.

Sauce Ingredients

- 2 tbsp margarine
- 3 tbsp flour
- 3/4 cup milk to cook scallops
- juice from lobster
- salt & pepper to taste
- 1/2 tsp celery salt

Sauce Directions

1. Cook sauce until thickened. Blend in 1 can cream of mushroom soup.

Main Directions

1. Thaw lobster and save juice for sauce.
2. Blanch scallops in milk approximately 5 minutes. Do not boil. Save milk for sauce.
3. Add scallops to sauce and blend in lobster, cooked rice, cut up hard boiled eggs, green peppers and sauted mushrooms.
4. Place ingredients in casserole dish and heat in oven at 350 degrees for 30-45 minutes.
5. Optional: Add grated cheese as a topping before heating.

Elmyra Lloyd lives in Hardwicke, NB and is well looked after by her caregiver, Halldis Wesenberg, who grew up in the Doucet Hennessy House and is a founding Board Member of the AMDHHA Inc.

Anna (Hennessy) and Henrik Wesenberg on their wedding day, June 1, 1946. This photo was taken on the lawn of the Doucet Hennessy House.

terri's spaghetti sauce

Submitted by Terri Jarratt

Ingredients

- Minced pork
- Onion
- Garlic
- Yellow pepper
- Orange pepper
- Mushrooms
- Celery
- Tomatoes
- Cayenne Pepper
- Olives (optional)

Barbara Hennessy, Harald Wesenberg and Theresa Jarratt (age 1), on the porch outside the Doucet Hennessy House, circa 1958.

Directions

1. In a large frying pan fry up as much minced pork as you want depending on how much sauce you plan to make.
2. Add onion, garlic, yellow pepper, orange pepper, mushrooms and celery. Dice them the size you want, stir fry the mixture together, cover and let steam.
3. While this is simmering, in a large pot boil up at least 6 tomatoes depending on how much sauce you want to make.
4. Steam meat and vegetables until tender and the tomatoes are mashable.
5. Then combine the meat mixture into the pot of cooked tomatoes and stir.
6. I use a large can of Catelli spaghetti meat sauce as a base but you can add any other type of spaghetti sauce to thicken it. Then add caynne pepper to taste. Beware, the more cayenne you put in, the hotter it gets.
7. Let the mixture simmer for about one hour and a half. Then enjoy! Olives are optional but they add a great flavour to the spaghetti sauce!!

boutilier veggie chowder

Submitted by Mannie (Odorico) Boutilier

Ingredients

Mannie and John Boutilier at
a Hawaiian night party in
CFS Shelburne, 1981.

- 30 oz clear chicken broth (preferably home made)
- 1 lb each of cauliflower and broccoli, cut up
- 5 slices bacon in 1/2 inch pieces
- 1 cup, chopped onion, red or spanish, or a mix of the two.
- 2 tbsp butter or margarine
- 1/4 cup all purpose flour
- 1/2 tsp salt
- 1/8 tsp pepper
- 2 1/2 cups evaporated milk
- 19 oz cream style corn

Directions

1. In a 4 Quart sauce pan over high heat, bring chicken broth, broccoli and cauliflower to a boil. Reduce heat and simmer for 10 minutes or until vegetables are tender.
2. Meanwhile, in a 12 inch skillet over medium heat, fry bacon until almost crisp.
3. Add onion and sauté for 5 minutes or until transparent.
4. Add butter or margarine, stir until melted. Stir in flour, salt and pepper. Cook and stir for 1-2 minutes.
5. Add milk, stir constantly and bring to a boil until thickened.
6. Next, pour mixture into pot with Broccoli and Cauliflower.
7. Add cream style corn, cover and cook over low heat for 15 minutes to blend flavours, stirring occasionally.
8. This makes 8 servings, about 1 1/3 cups per serving, but in my family of 4 it's a one meal deal.

A friend from Patsy Hennessy's Navy days, Manuela 'Mannie' Odorico Boutilier has kindly offered us one of her favourite recipes. Mannie is of Italian origin and her husband John Boutilier is French.

 63

acknowledgements

Like a good meal, many ingredients went into the making of this Recipe Book: / Comme tous bons repas, il a fallu beaucoup d'ingrédients pour achever cette première édition du Livre de Recettes:

Ingredients / Ingrédients

1. A pinch of good humour / Une pincée de bonne humeur

2. A dash of planning / Un soupçon de planification

3. Spoonfuls of editing / Plusieurs cuillerées d'édition

4. Buckets of cooperation / Des seaux de coopération

5. Translation as needed / Traduction au besoin

6. Contributions from friends and family to spice things up / Anecdotes de la part de la famille et des amis pour épicer le tout

Add measured doses of patience as well as the wisdom of our elders and ancestors and what you get is this unique fundraiser for the Association Doucet Hennessy House Association. / Ajouter la patience, la sagesse des anciens, et le tout produira une levèe de fonds sans pareil pour la Maison Doucet Hennessy Doucet Hennessy House Association.

Founding Board of Directors of the Association Maison Doucet Hennessy House Association Inc. Left to right: Rolande Doucet O'Connell, Michael Hennessy, Halldis Wesenberg, Melynda Jarratt and Patsy Hennessy (sitting). Photo taken in April, 2011. Photo courtesy of AMDHHA. / Conseil d'administration fondateur de l'Association Maison Doucet Hennessy House Association Inc. De gauche à droite: Rolande Doucet O'Connell, Michael Hennessy, Halldis Wesenberg, Melynda Jarratt et Patsy Hennessy (assise). Photo prise en avril 2011. Photo gracieuseté de AMDHHA.